Myths of
China and
JAPAN

Jen Green

**RAINTREE
STECK-VAUGHN
PUBLISHERS**

A Harcourt Company

Austin   New York
www.raintreesteckvaughn.com

Steck-Vaughn Company

First published 2002 by Raintree Steck-Vaughn Publishers, an imprint of Steck-Vaughn Company.

© 2002 Brown Partworks Limited

Library of Congress Cataloging-in-Publication Data

Green, Jen.
      Myths of China and Japan / Jen Green.
         p. cm. -- (Mythic world)
      Includes bibliographical references and index.
      ISBN 0-7398-4977-8

Printed and bound in the United States
1 2 3 4 5 6 7 8 9 0 IP 05 04 03 02 01

Series Consultant: C. Scott Littleton, Professor of Anthropology,
Occidental College, Los Angeles
Volume Author: Jen Green

for Brown Partworks Limited
Project Editor: Lee Stacy
Designer: Sarah Williams
Picture Researcher: Helen Simm
Indexer: Kay Ollerenshaw
Managing Editor: Tim Cooke
Design Manager: Lynne Ross
Production Manager: Matt Weyland

for Raintree Steck-Vaughn
Project Editor: Sean Dolan
Production Manager: Richard Johnson

Contents

General Introduction 4

The Story of Creation 6

August Personage of Jade 10

The Excellent Archer 14

How Yu Tamed the Waters 18

Empress of Heaven 22

The Creation of Japan 26

Izanagi Visits the Underworld 30

Amaterasu Hides the Daylight...34

Susano-wo and the Dragon's Sword 38

Okuninushi and Ninigi...42

Glossary...46

Further Reading and Viewing 47

Index...48

General Introduction

MYTHS ARE THE MIRRORS of humanity. They reflect the inner soul of a culture and try to give profound answers in a seemingly mysterious world. In other words, myths give the relevant culture an understanding of its place in the world and the universe in general. Found in all civilizations, myths sometimes combine fact and fiction and other times are complete fantasy. Regardless of their creative origin, myths are always dramatic.

Every culture has its own myths, yet globally there are common themes and symbols, even across civilizations that had no contact with or awareness of each other. Some of the most common types include those that deal with the creation of the world, the cosmos, or a particular site, like a large mountain or lake. Other myths deal with the origin of humans, or a specific people or civilization, or the heroes or gods who either made the world inhabitable or gave humans something essential, such as the ancient Greek Titan Prometheus, who gave fire, or the Ojibwa hero Wunzh, who was given divine instructions on cultivating corn. There are also myths about the end of the world, death and the afterlife, and the renewal or change of seasons.

The origin of evil and death are also common themes. Examples of such myths are the Biblical Eve eating the forbidden fruit or the ancient Greek story of Pandora opening the sealed box.

Above: *A 7th-century sculpture of Confucius, ancient China's most revered philosopher and teacher.*

Additionally there are flood myths, myths about the sun and the moon, and myths of a peaceful, beautiful place of reward, such as heaven or Elysium, or of punishment, such as hell or Tartarus. Myths also teach important human values, such as courage. In all cases, myths show

Above: *This 13th-century illustration shows a Japanese buddha, Jizo Bosatsu (left), rescuing souls from hell. Although Buddhism began in India, the Chinese and Japanese created stories about their own buddhas.*

that the gods and their deeds are outside of ordinary human life and yet essential to it.

In this volume some of the most important ancient Chinese and Japanese myths are presented. Following each myth is an explanation of how the myth was either reflected in or linked to the real life of either China or Japan. There is also a glossary at the end of the volume to help identify the major mythological and historical characters as well as explain many cultural terms.

MYTHOLOGY OF CHINA AND JAPAN

Historians believe that ancient Chinese mythology began around the 12th century B.C., and for more than 1,000 years afterward all the myths were passed down by word of mouth from generation to generation. Eventually the ancient myths became assimilated into the religious tales of the three major belief systems, Confucianism, Taoism, and Buddhism. In general, the supreme deity of Chinese mythology was the Jade

Emperor. He ruled over a large bureaucratic network of lesser deities whose responsibilities included running the day-to-day things on earth. This complicated structure in heaven actually imitated the real bureaucracy that existed in the Chinese emperor's imperial court.

Many ancient Chinese myths and mythological characters were influential in the development of the mythology of Japan, several hundred miles to the east. However, Shinto, the ancient religion of Japan, was unique to the island nation. Its mythology centers round Amaterasu, the sun goddess. Shinto stresses the harmony of humans with nature, and there are an infinite number of deities and spirits, called *kami*, that are believed to exist in all kinds of inanimate objects of nature, from rocks to streams. Some *kami* come from the souls of the dead, and eventually all souls become *kami*. In addition to the stories of Amaterasu and the other major deities, the adventures of the *kami* form the majority of Japanese myths.

The Story of Creation

For centuries many Chinese believed that the earth and heavens were created by a giant called Pan Ku and that a goddess named Nu Wa made the first humans.

IN THE BEGINNING only a confused, misty nothingness existed. It was shaped like an enormous egg. Gradually, a giant called Pan Ku emerged out of the nothingness. He decided to create the universe, so he made an ax and struck the egg-shaped mass, splitting it in two. All the dark, heavy forces of the mass, called the yin, sank down to become the earth, and all the bright, light elements, called the yang, rose up to become the heavens.

Fearing that the two halves of his creation would merge back into one, Pan Ku planted his feet firmly on the earth and pushed the heavens farther upward. For 18,000 years the giant kept pushing, until the earth and heavens were finally fixed in place. When Pan Ku died, his body changed to become the outer layer of the world as we know it. His back became the rugged mountains, his blood became the seas and rivers. The giant's breath turned into the wind, and plants sprouted from his skin. But his hair did not stay on earth. Instead it flew high into the heavens and became the millions of twinkling stars.

Now that the heavens and earth were created, more gods and goddesses came into being, but there were no humans. They were the work of a goddess named Nu Wa. Nu Wa's upper body looked human, but she had a serpent's tail. The goddess roamed the earth and found it beautiful but lonely. She longed for other beings who could appreciate all the wonders of nature that she saw.

Nu Wa's travels led her to the banks of the Yellow River in China. There she scooped up clay from the riverbank and fashioned it into a tiny figure. The top half of the figure resembled the upper part of the goddess's body, but the lower half had two legs instead of Nu Wa's serpent's tail. The goddess stood the figure on the bank and breathed life into it. Immediately it started laughing and dancing for joy at being alive.

Nu Wa made more people in the same way, but the work was slow and laborious. She decided to carry on creating humans using a quicker technique. The goddess took a vine, dipped it in mud, and whirled it around in a large circle. Each drop of mud that fell to the ground became a person. Some say that the humans Nu Wa made carefully by hand became rich and fortunate, and the drops of mud, which were far more numerous, became all the world's poor people.

Above: *The yin (earth) and yang (heavens) that the giant Pan Ku created are commonly represented as two halves rotating together inside a circle. The broken lines encircling the symbol also represent yin, and the unbroken lines, yang. Combined, it was believed, these symbols would drive off evil forces.*

Chinese Religions

In the past 2,500 years three major belief systems or religions have evolved in China. In general these religions do not compete with each other. Instead, the Chinese practice whatever elements of the major religions feel most suitable.

Archaeologists believe that around 3000 B.C., Chinese civilization began on the banks of the Yellow River (also known as the Huang Ho) — the site where Nu Wa made her clay figures — in northeastern China. The local people, called the Han, grew crops in the river valley, and built first villages, then towns, along the riverbanks. Civilization gradually spread southward across the neighboring plain to another river valley, along the Yangtze (also called the Cheng). The land of China came to be called "Zhong-guo," the Middle Kingdom, because the Chinese believed that it lay at the center of the world.

CHINESE BELIEF SYSTEMS

Beginning some 2,500 years ago three religions, or ways of living, took root in China: Confucianism, Taoism, and Buddhism. Most Chinese gods are of Taoist origin, but some myths draw on different beliefs. Confucianism, which is more a cultural approach to life than a set of spiritual beliefs, was founded by the philosopher K'ung Fu-tzu,

better known as Confucius, who was born in 551 B.C. and died in 479 B.C. Mainly concerned with practical matters and maintaining a high moral order within society, Confucianism stresses the importance of respecting one's ancestors, tradition, and the law.

Left: The founder of Confucianism, K'ung Fu-tzu (Confucius), laid the foundation for a belief system whose principles remain an important part of Chinese life. The teachings of Confucianism stress respect for social tradition and the maintenance of the relationship between just rulers and the ruled.

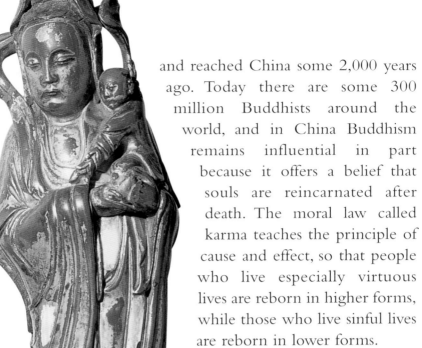

Taoism, founded around the same time as Confucianism, is a mystical religion. Followers of the Tao (which means "the way" and stands for the creation of everything) strive for perfection through harmony with nature and through balancing the forces of yin and yang. The teachings of the religion are based on two key texts, *Tao-te Ching* and *Chuang Tzu*. The most important Taoist myths come from two other books, *Travels in the West* and *Romance of the Investiture of the Gods*, both written during the Ming dynasty in the 15th century A.D.

The third major philosophical or religious movement, Buddhism, actually began in India in the 5th century B.C.

and reached China some 2,000 years ago. Today there are some 300 million Buddhists around the world, and in China Buddhism remains influential in part because it offers a belief that souls are reincarnated after death. The moral law called karma teaches the principle of cause and effect, so that people who live especially virtuous lives are reborn in higher forms, while those who live sinful lives are reborn in lower forms.

Left: *The Chinese Buddhist deity Kuan Yin, goddess of mercy and giver of children, is based on the Indian deity Avalokiteshvara.*

Yin and Yang

Taoists believe that two opposite and equal forces, yin and yang, underlie everything in the universe, with each containing the potential to create the other. Yin is considered cool, moist, dark, and feminine; yang is warm, dry, bright, and male. Yang can control yin when it grows dangerously excessive. In the creation story (see page 6), yin represents earth and yang stands for heaven. Together they create a balanced harmony.

Right: *Taoist philosophers study the yin-yang symbol in this 17th-century painting.*

August Personage of Jade

Yu Huang Shang-di is the most important Chinese god and ruler of the heavens. His name means "the August Personage of Jade," and he is also known as the Jade Emperor.

THERE ARE SEVERAL versions of the origin of Yu Huang, the Jade Emperor. Some claim that he was one of the first gods to have existed, others that he was one of three supreme deities. One legend states that he was born after his mother had a vision in which a holy man called Lao-tzu (a real person who is credited with founding the Taoist religion, see pages 8–9) handed her a child. In that same myth Yu Huang grew up to become a king, but later stepped down from his throne to study religion. As a holy man he attained perfection and at the moment of his death became an immortal god. Millions of years later he transformed into the Jade Emperor.

As the Jade Emperor, Yu Huang lived in the most beautiful palace in the highest level of heaven. He had a long wispy beard and wore a crown topped with a flat board hung with strings of pearls. His robes were embroidered with imperial dragons and he sat on a large throne.

Yu Huang was married to Xi Wangmu, who was also known as the Queen Mother of the West. Young and beautiful, she was often accompanied by a peacock. In her garden she grew a magical peach tree that bore fruit only once every 3,000 years. When the fruit ripened, the Queen Mother would host a banquet for the gods, at which the peaches were the main food. The magic peaches gave the gods immortality.

As ruler of the heavens, the Jade Emperor was too busy and important to have any direct involvement with affairs on earth. Instead he oversaw thousands of lesser gods and goddesses who were responsible for looking after the world and its inhabitants. Some deities were nature spirits in charge of lakes, rivers, and mountains; others were patrons of particular professions. For young men trying to pass the exams that led to lucrative administration careers with the imperial court, K'uei Hsing, the god of examinations, was the one they prayed to. There were also gods and goddesses who governed happiness, mercy, good fortune, and long life.

Each minor deity was in charge of a particular sector and had to report to their superiors once a month, and to the Jade Emperor once a year. If a deity's conduct was not satisfactory, he was dismissed and replaced by another god. Thus over time many divine offices were held by several gods.

Left: *The dress and style of leadership of Yu Huang, the Jade Emperor, was a model for the Chinese emperors on earth.*

Dynastic China

The Chinese believed their emperors to be appointed by heaven. As long as they ruled justly, good things would happen to the Chinese people. But when crops failed and natural disasters occurred, emperors could be deposed.

Early in China's history emperors took the title "Sons of Heaven" and modeled their courts on the heavenly court of the Jade Emperor (see page 10). The emperor, who lived a plush, sheltered life far removed from his subjects, was believed to be a deity on earth whose word was law. If, however, an emperor failed seriously in his duties he would lose the mandate of heaven and could be replaced by another nobleman who would begin a new dynasty — periods during which a particular family ruled China.

THE FIRST EMPEROR

Dynasties had ruled the country from long before the role of emperor began. The Shang were China's first great dynasty. They controlled northeastern China during the Bronze Age, from 1650 B.C. to 1027 B.C. They were followed by the Zhou (1027–256 B.C.), who established a feudal system whereby ordinary people were ruled by overlords. The Zhou era ended after a long civil war, and the Ch'in dynasty (221–207 B.C.), led by Emperor Cheng (259–210 B.C.), reunited the country.

Cheng, who called himself Shih Huang-ti, which means First Sovereign Emperor, was responsible for the style of leadership that subsequent emperors would imitate. He also began work on the Great Wall. The wall, which marks China's northern boundary and stretches 4,000 miles (6,400 km), was intended to keep out nomadic invaders.

Left: *Inside the tomb of Cheng, China's first emperor, 6,000 terra-cotta soldiers protected the dead ruler. The tomb, which covers 20 square miles (52 sq. km), was discovered in 1974, when local farmers uncovered the historic site while drilling a well.*

Left: *The imperial palace was the center of Chinese government and political power. When paying tribute to the emperor, thousands of officials would form a long procession into the palace courtyard and bow before him.*

During the Han dynasty (207 B.C.–A.D. 220), the emperors strengthened their control over China. They established a civil service, which was to govern the empire for the next 2,000 years. The emperor's civil service, like the heavenly court of the Jade Emperor, was a meticulously organized bureaucracy that ran the country like clockwork. Each department was headed by a senior minister who had scores of lesser officials to help him. Junior officers reported to their superiors, who in turn reported to higher-ranking officers, right up to those accountable to the emperor.

After a long period of unrest, the Sui ruled China from A.D. 589 to 618. Their greatest achievement was the canal that links the Yangtze and Yellow rivers.

During the Tang dynasty (618–906) China's economy prospered, and the arts, especially literature and music, flourished. When the Song dynasty

Below: *Although begun during the Ch'in dynasty, the Great Wall of China was reworked and strengthened in the 15th and 16th centuries, taking on the appearance we see today.*

(960–1279) took control they oversaw many advances in technology. Trade boomed under the Yuan (or Mongol) dynasty (1279–1368), and they were followed by the Ming (1368–1644), who were eventually replaced by the Qing (1682–1912).

By the beginning of the 20th century imperial rule had weakened, as Western nations began to exert greater influence in China. In 1912, the Qing dynasty and imperial rule in China ended for good when the Chinese military set up a republic.

The Excellent Archer

As in the ancient Greek myth of Zeus stopping Phaeton from scorching the earth, only the Chinese hero Yi, the divine archer, was able to prevent the 10 suns from burning the crops.

LONG, LONG AGO, the earth had not one but 10 suns. They were the children of the god Di Jun and his wife Xi He. Together they lived in the branches of a giant mulberry tree in the east. Each morning, one of the suns would rise and set off across the heavens, leaving his nine brothers in the tree; the next day, another sun would cross the sky. On earth, people thought there was only one sun.

After a thousand years of taking turns, the suns rebelled and all rose into the sky at once. On earth, temperatures grew hotter and hotter. Rivers dried up and rocks melted. But worst of all, the crops withered in the fields.

Yao, emperor of China, went to Di Jun and pleaded with him to recall his sons. "My people will starve unless you help us," the emperor cried. Di Jun summoned the divine archer, Yi, and asked him to deal with the problem. He gave Yi a strong bow and a quiver with 10 arrows — one for each sun.

Yi climbed a high crag and warned the suns to return home, but they took no notice. As they climbed higher in the sky, plains and forests were singed bare, and the land itself began to burn.

Yi strung his bow and fired an arrow straight at a sun. It exploded in a burst of light and fell to earth. Now Yi released a volley of arrows. One by one, the suns fell, and on earth temperatures grew cooler. Fearful that all the suns would die, the emperor crept up behind Yi, and stole one of his arrows. When Yi's quiver was empty, one sun still remained in the sky to light the world.

Di Jun was filled with sorrow at the death of his nine sons. Even though he had asked Yi to help, he now banished him and his wife, Zhang E, to earth. He condemned them to live and die like ordinary mortals. In despair, Yi went to Xi Wangmu, Queen Mother of the West, and asked for her help. Taking pity on him, the supreme goddess gave him the potion of immortality, which was made from her magic peaches. She told him to share it with his wife.

Yi returned home and told Zhang E the good news. But when he went out, his wife drank all the potion. The dose was too strong for one person and Zhang E's body became lighter than air. She floated upward all the way to the moon, where she now lives with a divine hare. You can still see Zhang E's hare if you look up at the full moon.

Above: *By shining on the same day, the 10 suns withered the crops and threatened to scorch the land. Yi, the excellent archer, shot down nine of them, leaving one to provide the right amount of sunlight.*

Climate and Farming in China

As the world's most populous country, China depends on the success of its agriculture. But throughout history the country's farmers have had to battle extreme weather conditions.

Today over a billion people live in China. Historically the country has always been heavily populated. With so many mouths to feed, farming has been a great priority. An old Chinese proverb explains that "The land is scarce and the people are many." A disaster like the drought caused by the 10 suns (see page 14) would have threatened China's ability to feed its people.

In 111 B.C., the Chinese emperor Wu Di declared: "Agriculture is the foundation of the world," and that farmers were to be respected for the job they performed in society. Even so, the farming life was still hard. Farmers toiled in the fields from dusk until dawn, yet had to pay heavy taxes and were expected to join the army in wartime. They also had to help with projects such as building public roads and waterways.

Above: *Farmers in southeastern China have tended the land the same way for centuries.*

Left: *Terraces used for rice paddies — flooded fields — have been cut into many mountainsides across the fertile province of Guangxi. Rice is the primary crop in the province, but in other eastern Chinese provinces wheat, sorghum, and cotton are most commonly grown.*

WORKING THE LAND

Despite China's huge size, only a relatively small part of the country is actually fertile farmland. In ancient times, eastern China was the most densely populated region because it was the most fertile. Farmers there cut steps of terraces into steep hillsides to make the most of what land there was, and spread ash and manure to fertilize the fields.

Rice is one of the main food crops in China, but it requires warm, wet growing conditions. In the humid south, it has been cultivated for over 6,000 years. Barley, wheat, and millet were grown in the yellow soil of the north. Hemp, cotton, tea, and fruits such as oranges, pears, litchi nuts, and cherries were also cultivated. Farmers kept pigs, ducks, geese, and chickens, and reared silkworms for silk.

In the dawn of China's history, farmers had only simple tools to work with, such as hoes, rakes, and sickles. By the 5th century B.C., oxen and buffalo were used to pull strong iron plows. In the 2nd century A.D., better horse harnesses were invented. Around the same time, farmers began to transport their goods to market by wheelbarrow.

During this era the Chinese also invented many new machines to help process grain. They ranged from pedal hammers for husking and water-driven hammers in mills, to hand-powered sifting or winnowing machines and water-mills for grinding grain.

Below: *A 2,000-year-old sculpture of a sheep pen from the Han dynasty.*

How Yu Tamed the Waters

Emperor Yao's long reign was troubled with many problems. After Yi had rid the earth of the rebellious suns, another powerful god, Tiandi, sent Gonggong to destroy mankind.

TIANDI, ONE OF THE gods of heaven, had grown tired of humans' wickedness, and the suffering that they caused each other. To rid the world of humans Tiandi ordered Gonggong, the god of water, to cause a great flood that would sweep across the land, destroy the crops, submerge the villages and towns, and drown all the people. When the floods began Yao again called on the gods to save his people. Gun, a god who often took the form of a white horse, heard the emperor's prayer.

Gun wandered the earth, trying to find a way of controlling the rising floodwaters. He met with an owl and a tortoise, who told him that a magic clay existed that would swell up when it came in contact with water. They suggested that the magic clay could be used to build a dam.

The clay was carefully guarded, but after many adventures, Gun finally succeeded in stealing a small amount. It was enough to build a giant dam that soon held the floods in check. When Tiandi saw what Gun had done, he became angry. He sent down a fire god who killed Gun and wrecked the dam. The floodwaters breached the barrier and surged back over the land.

But Gun's desire to help humankind was so strong that out of his body his son, Yu, was born. Yu, who could take the form of a dragon, continued his father's work. He labored hard to plug the 233,599 springs from which the floodwaters gushed. For 13 years he traveled the flooded kingdom, marking out the boundaries of China's nine provinces. Tiandi saw his efforts and, at last, his fierce heart softened. He allowed Yu to defeat Gonggong.

Using his strong dragon's tail, Yu gouged a series of deep furrows into the earth. These channels became China's great rivers, which discharged the swollen floodwaters into the sea. Yu then showed Emperor Yao and his people how to use the magic clay to build great dams and dikes that would protect low-lying areas from flooding.

In later years, Yu married, but did not tell his wife he was a god. One day, she came upon him when he was in the form of a bear. She fled in terror. Yu rushed after her to try to reassure her, but she died of fright. It was then that her son, Qi, was born from her body. Qi grew up to become one of China's wisest and mightiest emperors.

Above: *The god Yu used his magic powers to stop the floodwaters from covering the world. For the Chinese, floods from mighty rivers, such as the Yangtze, shown here, have always been real threats.*

China's Great Rivers

Myths about great floods that cover the earth are a feature of many different cultures. The Chinese had particular reason to fear the destructive power of floods.

The Yellow and Yangtze rivers are the two greatest rivers in eastern China. The Yellow River flows across northern China. The Yangtze divides the cool, dry north of China from the green, humid south.

Archaeologists believe that, around 3000 B.C., the valleys of these two great rivers were the birthplace of Chinese civilization. The ancient Chinese settled along the rivers because the soil there was ideal for farming. From time to time after heavy rain, the rivers burst their banks and spilled out over the surrounding plains. When the waters subsided, a rich, deep layer of fertile soil was left for farmers to cultivate crops.

During drier periods, the ancient Chinese peasants used river water to irrigate their fields and terraced hillsides. From around A.D. 1100, water was raised using a type of human-powered treadmill called an endless wheel. The endless wheel was operated by peasants who stood atop a large cogwheel and trod on pedals that turned the wheel and pumped water

upward. The Yangtze and Yellow rivers also acted as routes for shipping and were prime spots for fishing.

Centuries ago the Chinese began to build a network of waterways to extend the natural river systems. In the 6th century A.D., the Sui emperors embarked on an ambitious plan to dig a major canal that would link the Yangtze and Yellow rivers. The Grand Canal, as the artificial waterway became known, took 30 years to complete; during its construction, all men in China between the ages of 15 and 50 had to help with the digging.

Above: *Waterways, such as rivers and canals, are central to the economic well-being of many Chinese communities. This treadmill supplies water for irrigating nearby crops.*

Left: *The 13th-century artist Kaku Shukei painted this view of the Grand Canal some seven centuries after it was built.*

The finished canal stretched for 1,550 miles (2,500 km). It was used to transport soldiers across the empire, and to bring rice from the southeast to the imperial capital in the north.

CHINA'S SORROW

The Yangtze and Yellow rivers brought many blessings, but also terrible destruction. When the rivers burst their banks and floodwater surged over the lowlands, whole towns and villages were swept away and thousands drowned. The Yellow River was particularly treacherous, and even today it is known as "China's Sorrow," because of its terrible history of flooding. In 1938 a major flood from the river killed nearly a million people.

Building Flood Defenses

Throughout China's long history, successive emperors built dams and high dikes to control rivers. The river channels were also dredged to make them deeper, but to little effect. The flood defenses were always breached by the rivers at high water. Today a major new dam system is under way on the Yangtze, called the Three Gorges project. A new, giant dam is being built to protect the valley from flooding and to generate hydroelectricity. It is currently scheduled for completion in 2009. Over a million people have had to abandon their homes to make way for the huge reservoir that the new dam will create.

Right: *When it is completed in 2009 the enormous Three Gorges dam will help prevent flooding along the Yangtze.*

Empress of Heaven

Like the rest of the universe, the seas were under the general authority of the Jade Emperor, but several gods and goddesses protected sailors. The most popular was T'ien Hou, who was also called Empress of Heaven.

BEFORE SHE BECAME a goddess, T'ien Hou had been human. As a little girl, she lived on the island of Mei-chou. She had four brothers, who were all fishermen. One day each of her brothers set out in their own boats to cast their nets in various bays around the island. The young T'ien Hou remained at home.

The brothers had not been gone long when a great storm began brewing on the horizon. As the tempest swirled toward the island the skies darkened and huge waves crashed down on the little harbor town where T'ien Hou lived with her family. As the storm reached its height, the girl fainted and fell to the ground. Her family made many attempts to rouse her, but without success. Finally T'ien Hou's parents used a powerful stimulant to wake her. The girl slowly came round. She complained bitterly, saying that she had been woken too soon.

Eventually the storm passed and three of T'ien Hou's brothers sailed back into the harbor. As they scrambled ashore, each told the tale of how he had narrowly escaped death with the help of his little sister. Out at sea, as lightning crashed and thunder roared, giant waves had borne down on the brothers and threatened to swamp their little boats. Then, just when each brother thought all was lost, the spirit of T'ien Hou appeared, hovering above the water. Instantly the young girl calmed the waves, saving her brothers one after the other.

The fourth brother, however, never returned home. He drowned in the tempest because T'ien Hou had been woken before her spirit had time to reach his boat.

A few days later another violent storm struck the island. Just as before T'ien Hou fainted, but this time the young girl could not be roused and she died. Not long afterward local sailors reported that the girl's spirit had appeared to save them from the storm. From then on T'ien Hou's spirit returned to rescue sailors in every storm.

As her powers grew, T'ien Hou saved sailors from pirates and even ended deadly droughts by bringing rain. Her fame spread, and she was styled first princess, then queen, and finally empress of heaven. Sailors all over China carried statues of her in their boats to protect them from peril.

Above: *In modern-day Hong Kong a tall statue of T'ien Hou, the Empress of Heaven, overlooks Repulse Bay, protecting Chinese sailors from the dangers of the sea.*

Ships and Seafaring

From early times, the Chinese were a nation of expert sailors. Large and small vessels traveled rivers and coastal waters, braving dangers such as pirates and storms.

Left: *Working and traveling on waterways has been a part of everyday life in eastern China for centuries. During that time the small ferries and fishing boats seen here have changed little in design or function.*

The sea goddess is important to the Chinese because, for centuries, inland waterways and the seas around China have been used for transportation. Small, flat-bottomed wooden or bamboo craft bobbed about on canals and rivers. Simple boats called "sampans" (the name means "three planks") were often roofed by bamboo matting. Chinese sailors mostly propelled and steered their own crafts with a single oar at the stern.

At sea, larger, stouter craft — as well as the protection of T'ien Hou — were needed to brave rough waters and the fierce tropical storms, called typhoons, that often struck the region. Around A.D. 800, Chinese shipbuilders began to construct large wooden craft with several masts. By medieval times, large, flat-bottomed seafaring ships called junks had been developed. They carried up to six masts with huge, square sails made of woven matting.

compass, which was first discovered around A.D. 100 but not used regularly until around 1000, revolutionized navigation for Chinese sailors. The device meant sailors were able to cross the open ocean, out of sight of land.

Taking advantage of the greater distances mariners could travel, the 15th-century emperor Yong Le became interested in exploration. He sent a fleet to explore the South China Sea and the Indian Ocean.

Led by an admiral named Zheng He, a eunuch, and crewed by 27,000 sailors, the fleet made seven great journeys between 1405 and 1433. It explored Southeast Asian waters and crossed the Indian Ocean to Sri Lanka, India, Arabia, and the coast of East Africa.

Later emperors did not share Yong Le's desire to know what lay beyond China's borders. After the 15th century, China closed its borders and had little contact with the outside world until the 19th century.

Below deck, wooden bulkheads divided the ship's hold into many different compartments. This minimized the effect of leaks and helped the junk to stay afloat if it struck a reef in a storm.

During the 13th century, an Italian traveler named Marco Polo (1254–1324) visited China, where he was especially impressed by the huge size of Chinese junks. Up to 500 feet (150 m) long and 200 feet (60 m) wide, they were five times the size of the largest European vessels of the time. A strong rudder fitted to the stern made the junk relatively easy to maneuver, even in rough seas.

Above: A 19th-century painting of a 17th-century Chinese junk. For centuries junks were one of the world's largest types of shipping vessels.

Right: Marco Polo, shown here in a 16th-century fresco made some 250 years after his death, is credited with being the first European to explore China.

EXPLORING THE SEAS

The Chinese were not just building larger ships than the Europeans, they were also using the compass for navigation before them. The magnetic

The Creation of Japan

The Japanese islands cover millions of square miles off the east coast of Asia. Many Japanese believe their islands were created by a god called Izanagi and his wife, Izanami.

IN THE BEGINNING there were seven generations of powerful deities who each created a different part of the heavens and the universe. Izanagi and Izanami were of the youngest generation of gods. They grew up on Takamagahara, also known as the High Plain of Heaven, at a time when most of the universe had been fully formed. Only the earth, which was still unshaped and chaotic, was left to be made. The elder gods asked Izanagi and Izanami to complete the process of creation by molding the earth.

Izanagi and Izanami stood side by side on the floating bridge of heaven, which arched like a giant rainbow toward the unshaped planet, and spent much time contemplating how best to shape the earth. Eventually, Izanagi took the jeweled spear of heaven and dipped it into the misty waters that covered the earth. He stirred the waters several times and then lifted up the heavenly spear. A small drop of water fell from the tip of the spear. Where it hit, the water thickened and solidified to become the first dry land. The gods named the island Onogoro. (Many Japanese believe this ancient island lies somewhere in the sea near the islands of Japan. Today,

several islands claim the distinction of being Onogoro, but only the gods know which one is the real Onogoro.)

Izanagi and Izanami were so pleased with their creation that they descended to the island to make the place their home. They built a house and erected a sacred pillar in honor of the other gods. Next the two gods decided to join in marriage. They began the traditional ceremony by walking around the sacred pillar in opposite directions. After several turns round the pillar Izanami told her husband that he was most handsome of all the gods.

Though Izanami was merely paying her husband a compliment, she had broken protocol by speaking first in the marriage ritual — the man, not the woman, is supposed to speak first when getting married. Izanami's thoughtlessness greatly angered the other gods and they put a curse on the couple, so that their first offspring was born in the shape of a monstrous leech.

Izanagi and Izanami rejected the leech child, whom they named Hiruko. They abandoned him by casting him adrift in the ocean in a small reed boat. The child survived the dangers of the sea

Above: *The Japanese deities Izanagi and Izanami, the lovers who shaped the earth, are celebrated by the uniting of these large rocks, near Futamigaura, by an enormous marriage rope.*

and in time became known as Ebisu, god of fishermen and good fortune.

After they had sent away the leech child, Izanagi and Izanami became depressed. Taking pity on them, the other gods explained to the couple the mistake Izanami had made during the wedding ceremony. Now that they fully understood the proper way to perform the ritual they tried it again. This time they pleased the gods, and the couple's next children were born in more auspicious circumstances. Izanami gave birth to the other islands of Japan, and later to many more deities, including the gods of wind, the mountains, and the trees.

The Japanese Islands

Japan is made up of four large islands and thousands of small ones in the northwest Pacific. Although early on it was influenced by Korea and China to the west, Japan went on to develop its own distinctive culture and religion.

The largest island of Japan, Honshu, lies at the heart of the archipelago. Hokkaido, the next biggest island, sits to the north. The smaller islands of Shikoku and Kyushu lie southwest of Honshu, across the Inland Sea. The first land created by Izanagi and Izanami, Onogoro (see page 26), was also said to exist in the Inland Sea.

Together, the archipelago of Japan forms an arc that stretches 1,200 miles (1,900 km) from north to south. Northern Hokkaido lies as far north as Quebec in Canada, southern Kyushu as far south as the Gulf of Mexico. This huge north–south distance means that the Japanese islands have very different climates and vegetation. Northern

Left: *Mount Fuji is Japan's tallest mountain, reaching 12,388 feet (3,776 m) high. Like many mountains in Japan, it is considered a sacred site.*

Hokkaido has a cold climate similar to Scandinavia, with long, freezing winters and subarctic vegetation. Southernmost areas have a balmy, subtropical climate with lush vegetation.

Inland, most of Japan is occupied by steep, craggy mountains covered with dense forests. Swift-flowing streams have gouged deep ravines through the mountains, but the only nearly flat land lies near the coasts. In ancient times, settlements grew up in coastal areas, but the rugged terrain made inland travel very difficult. Travelers journeyed around the coast and crossed to other islands by boat.

Because travel was restricted by the sea and the high mountain ranges on each of the main islands, the peoples developed different traditions and lifestyles. Northerners were said to be patient and hardy, southerners were thought to be great fighters. The people of central Honshu were said to value glory above all things.

Above: *The climate in the islands of southwest Japan is generally warm and subtropical, very different from the climate in the north.*

EARLY SETTLERS

Japan has a very ancient history, stretching back tens of thousands of years. The first settlers from the Asian mainland are thought to have arrived around 30,000 B.C. By 10,000 B.C., the first civilization, called the Jomon culture, was developing on Honshu's coastal plains. The Jomon were hunter-gatherers who collected shellfish and hunted animals in the forests. Isolated from the Asian mainland, they developed a distinctive culture and religion.

The Jomon worshiped spirits whom they believed resided in springs, rivers, crags, and other natural features. Over time, these beliefs developed into Shinto, Japan's indigenous religion.

Some time after 300 B.C., more settlers arrived in Japan from China and Korea and introduced what is called the Yayoi culture. They brought with them new metalworking skills and showed the Jomon how to grow rice. Gradually the first villages grew up, and ancient Japan became a network of small states, ruled over by clan chiefs. By the 5th century, one clan, the Yamato, had grown more powerful than all others. Their descendants became emperors of Japan (see pages 44–45).

Left: *An earthenware bowl dating from the ancient Jomon culture on Japan.*

Izanagi Visits the Underworld

Izanami's last child was Kagutsuchi, god of fire. In giving birth to him, the goddess was so badly burned that she died and was sent to live in Yomi, the dark, gloomy underworld.

IZANAGI WAS OVERCOME with grief at his wife's death and blamed his newborn son, Kagutsuchi, for causing her to die. He grew so angry with the infant that he took a sword and cut off the baby's head. Immediately several new gods and goddesses emerged from Kagutsuchi's body. On realizing the horrible thing he had done, Izanagi became ridden with guilt and cried harder than ever. From his tears grew more deities.

When Izanami died her spirit had been sent to Yomi, the underworld kingdom of the dead. For many days Izanagi felt lost without his wife. Eventually he decided to journey to the underworld kingdom to bring her back. The god traveled deep into Yomi before he finally found Izanami's spirit. He explained to the spirit of his wife that he was there to take her home, but she said that she could not return to the land of the living because she had eaten the food of the dead. Only the God of Death could release her.

Izanagi vowed to enter the dark hall of the God of Death to plead with him to release his beloved wife's spirit. Although Izanami's spirit urged her husband not to enter the hall, Izanagi would not listen to her.

Izanagi marched into the hall but could not see his way through the darkness. Using one of the teeth from his hair comb, he made a flaming torch that shone light everywhere. Immediately screams of death boomed throughout the hall and he found himself standing over a decaying corpse. It was the lifeless body of Izanami. Izanagi recoiled in horror and fled the hall.

Abandoned and humiliated, Izanami's spirit sent demons, called the hags of Yomi, chasing after Izanagi. With the hags hot on his heels, Izanagi threw down first his headdress, which turned into grapes, then his comb, which became bamboo shoots. Each time the hags stopped to eat the food, Izanagi got further ahead.

Near the entrance to Yomi, Izanami's spirit changed into one of the hags and came screaming toward him. Izanagi rolled a huge boulder against the entrance to seal it forever.

Back in the land of the living, Izanagi recovered from his ordeal. His body felt polluted by the dust of Yomi, and he decided to bathe. He stripped off his clothes and washed in the Hi River. Each time he scrubbed off some of the dust from Yomi a new deity was born.

Above: *Yomi, the underworld of the dead, was ruled by the God of Death, shown here, in this 19th-century painting, sitting on his throne and overseeing the horrors of the afterlife.*

Finally, he washed his face, which gave birth to the three greatest deities. Washing his left eye, Izanagi gave birth to Amaterasu, the sun goddess. The moon god, Tsuki-yomi, was born from Izanagi's right eye, and the storm god, Susano-wo, from his nose.

Now Izanagi decided to divide the universe between his three new children. He gave the eldest, Amaterasu, five strings of jewels and rule over the heavens, he made Susano-wo god of the oceans, and he presented Tsuki-yomi with the kingdom of the night.

Religion in Japan

Shinto, Confucianism, and Buddhism have been practiced in Japan for centuries. Shinto, which originated in Japan, was influenced by the other two religions, which came from Asia.

Traditionally the Japanese are a very devout and religious people. Until 1945 Shinto was the official religion in Japan. Shinto, a name that means "the way of the gods," is a very ancient religion, dating back thousands of years to Jomon times (see page 29), and Izanagi's children, Amaterasu, Tsuki-yomi, and Susano-wo, are the principal Shinto deities (see pages 30–31). As well as these and other major figures, there are literally millions of lesser deities called spirits or *kami*, such as those that emerged from Izanagi when he bathed.

Snow-capped mountains, rivers, seas, ancient trees, and other natural wonders all contain *kami*. It was believed that all people, from shogun to peasant, became *kami* when they died.

Praying or paying homage to *kami* is meant to keep the spirits happy, so the Japanese built shrines up and down the country for regular worship. Entering through a ceremonial gateway called a *torii*, worshipers wash to purify themselves before praying, just as Izanagi does after leaving Yomi.

There are two main groups of *kami*, heavenly and earthly spirits. Once, the gods had moved freely between heaven and earth using a bridge, but eventually it collapsed into the sea and those stuck on earth remained there. All *kami* are essentially good, but they have two souls, one gentle and one violent. They can bring disaster and misfortune if their violent soul gets the upper hand, so they have to be appeased through prayer.

Below: *A Shinto priest performs ritual prayers to the* kami *at a shrine.*

Above: *This 9th-century* torii *gate marks the sacred entrance to a Shinto shrine at Miyajima, near Hiroshima.*

Shinto encourages respect for nature and reverence for, even worship of, one's ancestors. It also stresses the importance of ritual and tradition. Before World War II, it emphasized allegiance to Japan and the emperor.

OTHER BELIEFS

As well as Shinto, Confucianism and Buddhism are important religions in Japan, both having spread to the islands from mainland Asia. Buddhism became popular in Japan in the late 6th century A.D., having arrived from Korea. It has been practiced side by side with Shintoism ever since. In medieval times, Zen Buddhism, a form of Buddhism that stresses the importance of meditation, became popular among the samurai, or warrior class.

Arriving in Japan around the same time as Buddhism, Confucianism greatly influenced the more mystical Shinto belief system. Even today, most Japanese people practice a mix of the major religions, with Shinto rituals being performed at births and marriages and Buddhist ceremonies used most often for funerals.

Sources of Japanese Myths

The stories about Izanagi and his three major children — Amaterasu, Tsuki-yomi, and Susano-wo — are very ancient. Before the Japanese developed a written script, they and other myths were handed down by word of mouth. At the beginning of the 8th century A.D., Empress Gemmyo commissioned scholars to produce a written anthology of Shinto legends and a history of Japan. The anthology, entitled *Kojiki* ("The Record of Ancient Matters"), was completed in 712, and the *Nihon Shoki* ("Chronicles of Japan") in 720. The books are the main sources of Japanese myths.

Above: *The drum and text represent the music of the gods performed at Shinto rituals.*

Amaterasu Hides the Daylight

Amaterasu and Tsuki-yomi settled down to rule the realms of day and night, as their father, Izanagi, had ordered. Only Susano-wo, the storm god, was unhappy with his realm. He set out to stir up trouble among his siblings.

SUSANO-WO, THE GOD OF STORMS, climbed to Takamagahara, or the High Plain of Heaven, where his father, Izanagi, had been raised (see page 26). There he challenged his sister, Amaterasu, the sun goddess, to a miracle-working contest. Amaterasu took her brother's sword, broke it into three pieces, and used them to create three goddesses. In reply, Susano-wo took Amaterasu's five strings of jewels and used them to create five male deities. Each claimed victory in the contest.

Frustrated by not being declared the outright winner, Susano-wo became increasingly wild and destructive. He summoned storms and wrecked the rice fields that his sister had planted on earth. Finally, he threw a dead pony into the hall where she was peacefully weaving with her women helpers. Amaterasu fled in terror and shut herself up in a rocky cave.

Amaterasu's disappearance plunged the earth into darkness and perpetual winter. All the crops failed, and under the cover of darkness, evil spirits performed wicked deeds. The other gods decided that the situation could not continue. They gathered around Amaterasu's cave and tried to lure her out with sounds of music and merry-making. But the sun goddess was so frightened that she refused to budge.

Then some of the gods came up with a plan. They hung a magic mirror and a string of jewels on a tree outside the cave. Then Ama-no-Uzume, a dawn goddess, climbed onto an upturned tub and began to dance to the music. She drummed her feet to the rhythm, and then with everyone staring lifted her dress and pulled down her underwear. The gods roared with laughter.

Amaterasu peeped from the cave to find out what all the laughter was and caught sight of herself in the mirror. Convinced that another sun goddess had appeared, she came a little way out of the cave. The gods seized her and roped off the cave so she could not get inside again. Reluctantly, Amaterasu agreed to return to the realm of heaven. In this way, sunlight and life-giving warmth were restored to the world.

On another occasion, Amaterasu sent Ukemochi, the food goddess, to her other brother, Tsuki-yomi. Ukemochi invited the moon

Above: *This woodblock print from 1860 depicts the moment when Amaterasu, the sun goddess, emerges from the cave in which she had been hiding following the attacks of her brother Susano-wo.*

god for a meal, then produced a banquet of rice and other dishes from her nose and mouth and even her anus. Disgusted at food produced in this way, Tsuki-yomi destroyed Ukemochi. At once new types of food, including rice, millet, wheat, red beans, and soybeans, sprouted from her body.

When Amaterasu discovered that Tsuki-yomi had killed Ukemochi, the sun goddess vowed never to see her brother again. However, she did allow the new crops to be cultivated by the people of Japan so that they could grow a greater and more abundant variety of food.

Farming in Japan

Amaterasu, the Shinto sun goddess, is the principal deity in Japanese mythology. Her status reflects the importance of the sun and its effect on a good harvest.

Amaterasu is worshiped all over Japan, but her main shrine stands at Ise in central Honshu. Considering that the sun goddess is the primary deity in Shinto mythology, it may appear surprising that her main shrine is a simple wooden structure shaped like a grain store. Yet the shape of the building serves as a reminder of the sun's importance in producing much needed crops for food.

Japan was traditionally a fishing and agricultural society, and followers of Shinto, of which there are still many, pray regularly for good harvests. Besides Amaterasu, the deity prayed to most often for ample crops is Ukemochi, the food goddess. The story about Ukemochi (see pages 34–35) is similar to myths from many cultures around the world that link crops and the harvest with the sacrificial death of a deity.

In around 300 B.C., the Japanese abandoned hunting and gathering, and settled down to farming. One of the main crops they grew was rice. Other important crops included wheat, millet, red beans, and soybeans, all mentioned

in the myth of Ukemochi. Vegetables, such as radishes and sweet potatoes, and many types of fruit were also grown.

Rice cultivation requires moist conditions and intensive farming methods. The crop was often grown in flooded fields called rice paddies, where carp fish were also kept for food. All over Japan, hillsides were stepped into little terraces to make maximum use of the land that could be farmed. In

Above: *The sacred Shinto shrine at Ise dedicated to the sun goddess, Amaterasu. It was originally built in the 3rd century A.D. and has been ritually rebuilt every 20 years.*

Left: *This 19th-century illustration of the Yokohama customhouse, one of the world's most famous ports at the time, shows merchant sailors having their goods weighed and valued. Rice was a chief Japanese export.*

spring, farmers painstakingly planted neat rows of rice seedlings on the muddy terraces. Whole families stood knee deep in cold water for long hours to carry out this backbreaking work.

As in China, farmers were respected but lived a hard life. Most peasants did not own the land they worked but rented it from landlords. A large part of their harvest went straight to the landlord in tax, and they were not free to leave the land. This situation continued, more or less, into the 19th century, when it was virtually abolished. After World War II further land reforms were introduced, and many more farmers were able to buy land.

SOCIAL STATUS OF FARMERS

Japanese society was traditionally divided into four main classes. The samurai, or warrior, class had the highest status. Next came farmers who produced food, and craftsmen who

Left: *This Japanese farmer is planting rice shoots in a paddy field. For centuries farmers in Japan have used the same effective methods of cultivating rice.*

made useful tools and weapons. Merchants were considered the lowest class because they did not actually produce anything. However, in later years merchants were often better off than farmers because they made a good profit through trade.

Susano-wo and the Dragon's Sword

Although Susano-wo was the god of storms and thunder, he was not always wicked. In this myth he rids the world of an evil dragon and discovers a magical sword that would later be prized by emperors of Japan for centuries.

THE OTHER GODS DECIDED to punish Susano-wo after his poor treatment of Amaterasu, which had forced the sun goddess to take refuge in a cave (see page 34). The gods cut off the storm god's beard, pulled out his toenails and fingernails, and banished him from heaven.

Forced to wander the earth, Susano-wo traveled alone for many years until, in the Izumo region of western Japan, he met with an elderly couple and their young daughter, Kusa-nada-Hime. All three were weeping. When Susano-wo asked what was wrong, the old man told him that Kusa-nada-Hime was the only survivor of their eight daughters. The other seven girls had been killed by a terrible dragon called Yamata-no-Orochi. The dragon, which had eight heads and eight tails, had only been hunting in the region for a few days. Now their last child was set to be killed by the dragon too.

Susano-wo told the couple that he was the brother of Amaterasu, the sun goddess. In recognition of his importance the couple promised to give him their daughter if he could defeat the dragon. Susano-wo prepared eight huge vats of rice wine, or sake, and settled down to wait for Yamata-no-Orochi. When the dragon appeared, the smell of the wine drew it straight to the vats, and all eight heads drank deeply. The dragon quickly became drunk and fell into a deep sleep.

Susano-wo saw his chance and cut off all eight of the dragon's heads, one by one. Then he cut the dragon's body to pieces and finally he chopped up the eight tails. In one of the dragon's middle tails, he found a gleaming, magical sword that would later feature in many legends.

The sword would be called Kusanagi, which means "the grass-mower," because of an adventure in which a hero used it to cut down the high grass that was hiding his enemy. Over the years Kusanagi's fame grew, and the sword became one of the emblems of the Japanese emperors. It is now said to be housed in a temple near the town of Nagoya in central Honshu.

As for Susano-wo, he married Kusa-nada-Hime, and the couple moved into a palace near the town of Suga. There they lived happily, and Kusa-nada-Hime gave birth to a daughter, Suseri-Hime.

Above: *In one of the eight tails of Yamata-no-Orochi, the evil dragon, Susano-wo discovered Kusanagi, the sword that would feature in many legendary Japanese adventures.*

Swords and Samurai

The many adventures of the dragon's sword, known as Kusanagi, shows how highly prized swords were among the Japanese. This was especially true for members of the elite warrior class that emerged in medieval times — the samurai.

The medieval period of Japanese history is a long chronicle of civil war and bloodshed. For centuries, Japan's most powerful clans waged war almost constantly on one another to gain territory and influence over the emperor. Clan chiefs called *daimyo* hired armies of samurai — the word means "one who serves" — to fight on their behalf. These warriors pledged allegiance to their lord and vowed to defend his interests at all costs.

By the 12th century, the samurai had developed a complex code of conduct called *bushido*, which means "the way of the warrior." The code placed a warrior's honor above life itself. The ultimate consequence of the code meant that instead of conceding defeat, a samurai would commit ritual suicide — called *seppuku* — by first slicing open his own belly before another samurai ended his agony by cutting off his head.

In battle the samurai wore heavy armor made of strips of metal and leather bound together with silk. Their

stout helmets bore terrifying emblems designed to strike fear in the hearts of their enemies. Originally, the samurai mainly fought on horseback, using bows and arrows; in later years, they became expert swordsmen. Only

Above: *A master swordsmith at work on a* katana.

members of the highly respected warrior class were allowed to carry the long, curved swords called *katana*.

FORGING THE SWORD

A samurai's sword was his most prized possession. The finest weapons were precious heirlooms handed down from father to son. A samurai sword took long hours of painstaking work to make, as the metal blade was coated with many thin layers of the hardest steel and then honed to razor-sharpness. Not surprisingly, the smiths who produced the weapons were regarded as master craftsmen, and their work took on a spiritual dimension. Before starting a new sword, the smith would fast to purify himself, as if embarking on a religious quest. And while working at his forge, the smith would wear a monk's robe.

When the samurai's sword was finished, it was tested on a corpse — or sometimes on a living person of low

Above: *This scroll illustrates one of the first battles between samurai, at Sanjo Palace in 1159.*

status — using a series of strokes that were performed in ascending order of difficulty. The first cut was intended to severe the hand at the wrist; the most difficult to slice the whole body in two with a single stroke.

In the early 17th century, Japan entered a more settled period, and wars became less frequent. The samurai used the centuries of peace that followed to hone their fighting skills into ritual arts. As time went on, they became more interested in peaceful pursuits, such as tea drinking and being bureaucrats, than in mortal combat. Despite its benevolent activities, the samurai class was abolished in the late 19th century.

Below: *Expert blacksmiths were employed to make armor for samurai.*

Okuninushi and Ninigi

Legends claim that the province of Izumo in western Japan had several famous rulers. One was Okuninushi, god of medicine and healing. Another was Ninigi, whose descendants became emperors of Japan.

OKUNINUSHI HAD 80 brothers who were all jealous of him, and once he had grown up they tried to kill him. After a narrow brush with death, the young man decided to take refuge in the village of Suga. There he met and fell in love with Suseri-Hime, daughter of Susano-wo and Kusa-nada-Hime.

The young girl was kind and invited the stranger to sleep at her family's palace. At first the storm god refused to allow the stranger to stay, but after Suseri-Hime pleaded with her father, he agreed. But secretly he was suspicious of Okuninushi and set a series of traps to get rid of the unwelcome suitor.

On the first night of his stay, Susano-wo made Okuninushi sleep in a room filled with poisonous snakes, and on the second night, in a room full of wasps and centipedes. Each time Suseri-Hime gave Okuninushi a magic scarf that protected him from harm.

On another occasion, Susano-wo sent the hero into the middle of a giant meadow to fetch an arrow, then set fire to the grass. Okuninushi was saved by a mouse that retrieved the arrow and showed him an underground chamber where he could hide from the flames.

Okuninushi decided to steal away with Suseri-Hime. One night when Susano-wo was asleep Okuninushi tied the storm god's hair to the rafters and then escaped with Suseri-Hime. Susano-wo woke up and, while trying to release himself, pulled down the whole palace. He emerged from the rubble and pursued the fleeing couple, but the young lovers managed to escape.

Far away from Suga, Okuninushi and Suseri-Hime married and settled down to rule the kingdom of Izumo. But Okuninushi's brothers, who were still jealous, waged war on him, and the province was reduced to chaos.

Amaterasu, the sun goddess, decided to intervene and placed her own grandson, Ninigi, on the throne of Izumo. Okuninushi was forced to abdicate when Ninigi appeared bearing three divine gifts that proved he was Amaterasu's grandson. The gifts were the heavenly jewels, the mirror that the gods had used to lure Amaterasu from the cave (see page 34), and the sword later named Kusanagi (see page 38). These three

Above: *At the Jinushi shrine in Kyoto, this wooden sculpture and sign honor Okuninushi for being the protector of love and good or suitable unions and for having a kind heart and giving happiness to everybody.*

treasures later became the symbols of Japanese imperial power.

Ninigi married the daughter of a mountain god, but when his young wife became pregnant not long after the wedding, he suspected her of being unfaithful. The young bride was determined to prove her innocence. When the time came for her to give birth, she shut herself inside a house without doors or windows and then set fire to it, declaring that she would die if she had been unfaithful. Instead of being burned to death, she survived and bore triplets, all boys. One of the boys became the founder of the Yamato imperial line of Japan.

The Emperors of Japan

The Yamato family have sat on the imperial throne of Japan for over 1,500 years. Yet for many centuries they were forced to be subservient to the families that controlled the office of shogun.

When the Yamato family began their long, warring conquest of Japan in around A.D. 330, the country was made up of rival clans and small states. The wars finally ended in the later 4th and early 5th centuries with the unification of the country and the beginning of the Yamato imperial line.

Historians believe that the myth of Ninigi taking the Izumo throne from Okuninushi (see pages 42–43) is based on the ancient victory of the Yamato

Left: *Akihito, the emperor of Japan (third left), and the royal family greet a flag-waving crowd. Akihito ascended the throne in 1989, and he in turn will be succeeded by his eldest son, Naruhito (second left), who was born in 1960.*

clan over its rivals. The Yamato worshiped Amaterasu, the sun goddess, while their main rivals paid homage to Susano-wo, the storm and sea god. After they were victorious the Yamato clan not only made Amaterasu the principal deity of the new empire but also claimed her as their own ancestor.

From that time on Japanese emperors were regarded as living gods, descendants of the sun goddess. In recognition of their divine ancestor, the rising sun became the national emblem. It still appears on the Japanese flag.

EMPEROR AS GOD

As in China, the Japanese emperor was believed to have a mandate from heaven and was considered a living deity. Whenever the emperor appeared in public, ordinary people were supposed to hide indoors or bow down low enough to avoid looking at his face.

But following Japan's defeat in World War II, Emperor Hirohito (1901–1989) was forced by the Allies to declare that he was not a living god. Today the emperor's role is largely ceremonial, similar to that of European monarchs.

The Shogun vs. the Emperor

Although the reign of the emperors stretches back some 1,500 years, for most of that time Japan was governed by military leaders called "shogun." The title means "barbarian-quelling generalissimo," and the position was originally that of chief military commander. Toward the end of the 12th century, as the feudal system was ripping the kingdom apart, the shogun defeated the feudal lords and, with the backing of the army, wrested control from the emperor. During the 13th and early 14th centuries, the Minamoto clan ruled Japan as shoguns. They were followed by the Ashikaga shogunate (1338–1573), and from 1603 to 1868, the title was held by the Tokugawa family. In 1868, Emperor Meiji succeeded in winning power from the shoguns, with the backing of other noble families, and reasserted imperial control over Japan.

Left: *Minamoto Yoritomo (1147–1199), the first shogun, although ruthless and murderous, proved a skilled administrator.*

Glossary

Amaterasu The sun goddess, daughter of **Izanagi** and supreme **Shinto** deity.

Ama-no-Uzume In Japanese mythology, a dawn goddess who lured **Amaterasu** out of her cave, restoring sunlight to the world.

Buddhism An ancient religion that originated in India and spread to both China and Japan. It teaches a belief in reincarnation and that its followers should lead virtuous lives.

bushido Code of conduct for the **samurai** that emphasized honor above one's own life.

Cheng (259 B.C.–210 B.C.) Chinese emperor who began the Great Wall of China. Also called Shih Huang-ti.

Confucianism An ancient Chinese belief system, founded by K'ung Fu-tzu (551 B.C.–479 B.C.), also known as Confucius, that teaches, among other things, the importance of tradition.

Di Jun In Chinese mythology, a god who had 10 sons, each a sun.

Gemmyo An 8th-century Japanese empress who ordered the documenting of **Shinto** legends.

Gonggong In Chinese mythology, the god of water who tried to destroy humans by flooding the earth. He was stopped by **Yu**.

Gun The god who tried to stop **Gonggong** from flooding the earth.

Hiruko The first son of **Izanagi** and **Izanami**. He was born a leech child and became known as Ebisu, god of fishermen and good fortune.

Izanagi Father of Japan, husband to **Izanami**, and creator of the three major deities, **Amaterasu**, **Tsuki-yomi**, and **Susano-wo**.

Izanami Wife to **Izanagi** and mother of Japan. She died giving birth to Kagutsuchi.

Izumo Province in western Japan from where the imperial family, **Yamato**, emerged.

Jomon Japan's first civilization, which began around 10,000 B.C.

junk A large seafaring sailing ship, similar to a Spanish galleon.

kami In **Shinto** religion the lesser gods, who include the spirits of ancestors. They exist in inanimate objects such as rocks, trees, and streams.

Kusa-nada-Hime In Japanese mythology, the wife of **Susano-wo** and mother of **Suseri-Hime**.

Kusanagi The sword pulled out of the tail of the dragon **Yamata-no-Orochi**; one of the emblems of the Japanese emperors.

Lao-tzu The founder of **Taoism** in the 6th century B.C.; he appeared to **Yu Huang**'s mother in a dream heralding the god's birth.

Ninigi Grandson of **Amaterasu** and ancestor of the **Yamato** dynasty.

Nu Wa In Chinese mythology, an early goddess, half-serpent and half-woman, who created humans.

Okuninushi Husband of **Suseri-Hime** and ruler of **Izumo** province before **Ninigi**.

Onogoro The first island created by **Izanagi** and **Izanami**. Its exact location is disputed.

Pan Ku In Chinese mythology, a giant who created the **yin** (earth) and the **yang** (heavens).

sampan Small wooden Chinese boat, often with a bamboo roof.

samurai Japanese elite warriors or mercenaries.

seppuku A type of ritual suicide performed by **samurai**.

Shinto An ancient Japanese belief system. The religion encourages respect for nature and one's ancestors, among other things.

shoguns Military leaders who held the real power in Japan, from the 12th to the 19th centuries.

Susano-wo The storm god and son of **Izanagi**. He had many adventures, including forcing his sister, **Amaterasu**, into a cave, defeating the terrible dragon **Yamata-no-Orochi** and discovering **Kusanagi**.

Suseri-Hime The daughter **Susano-wo**, she became the wife of **Okuninushi**. They ruled **Izumo** together before **Ninigi**.

Takamagahara Also known as the High Plain of Heaven, it was where **Izanagi** and **Izanami** were raised. It was also the place from where **Amaterasu** ruled the heavens.

Taoism An ancient Chinese mystical religion that teaches its followers to strive for perfection through harmony with nature.

Tiandi In Chinese mythology, a chief god who ordered **Gonggong** to flood the world.

T'ien Hou In Chinese mythology, a young girl whose spirit saved sailors from drowning. She is also known as the Empress of Heaven.

torii The ceremonial gateway entrance to a **Shinto** shrine.

Tsuki-yomi The moon god and son of **Izanagi**.

Ukemochi In Japanese mythology, the food goddess who was destroyed by **Tsuki-yomi**. Out of her body came the first crops of new grains, such as rice and wheat.

Wu Di An ancient Chinese emperor who declared the importance of agriculture.

Xi He In Chinese mythology the wife of **Di Jun**.

Xi Wangmu The wife of **Yu Huang**, she was also called Queen Mother of the West.

Yamata-no-Orochi In Japanese mythology, the terrible dragon that was killed by **Susano-wo**. Out of its tail was pulled **Kusanagi.**

Yamato The imperial family of Japan. They are believed to be descended from **Amaterasu** and **Ninigi**, and have ruled Japan for over 1,500 years.

Yao In Chinese mythology, an ancient emperor who pleaded with the gods to save the world.

Yayoi The Japanese civilization, which originated in China and Korea, that overtook the ancient **Jomon** in around 300 B.C.

Yi In Chinese mythology, the divine archer who shot down nine of the 10 suns and saved the crops.

yin & yang The essence of the universe, with the earth being yin and the heavens, yang. It is believed that these two forces are equal and that when joined together they create a balanced harmony.

Yomi In Japanese mythology, the underworld, or the place where the spirits of the dead live.

Yu In Chinese mythology, the son of **Gun** and the one who stopped **Gonggong** from flooding the earth.

Yu Huang Also known as the Jade Emperor, the ruler of the heavens and chief god in the Chinese pantheon.

Zen Buddhism A form of **Buddhism** that emphasizes mental meditation. It is popular in Japan and in many other places around the world.

Zheng He A 15th-century Chinese admiral who explored as far as the east coast of Africa.

Further Reading & Viewing

BOOKS

Allan, Tony, et al. *Realm of the Rising Sun: Japanese Myth.* Alexandria, VA: Time Life, 1999.

Mann, Elizabeth. *The Wonders of the World Book: The Great Wall.* Buffalo, NY: Mikaya Press, 1997.

Matthews, R. *Myths and Civilization of the Ancient Chinese.* Lincolnwood, IL: NTC/Contemporary, 2000.

Netzley, Patricia D. *Modern Nations of the World: Japan.* San Diego, CA: Lucent Books, 2000.

Paludan, Ann. *Chronicle of the Chinese Emperors.* New York, NY: Thames and Hudson, 1998.

Sokyo, Dr. Ono. *Shinto: The Kami Way.* Boston, MA: Charles E. Tuttle Co., 1994.

VIDEOS

Biography: Confucius. A&E Video, 1996.

Religions: Shinto. Schlessinger Media, 1999.

Shogun: Supreme Samurai. A&E Video, 2001.

Touring China. Questar, 1998.

WEBSITES

Chinese Mythology. http://www.windows.ucar.edu/cgi-bin/tour_def/mythology/china_culture.html.

Japanese Mythology. http://www.interq.or.jp/www-user/fuushi/e-myth-a.htm.

Shinto: Schauwecker's Guide to Japan. http://www.japan-guide.com/e/e2056.html.

Index

Page numbers in *italics* refer to picture captions.

Akihito, Emperor *44*
Ama-no-Uzume 34
Amaterasu 5, 31, 32, 34, *36*, 42, 45
archer, divine (Yi) 14, *15*

Buddhism 9, 33
bushido 40

Cheng, Emperor *12*
China
    climate and faming *16–17*
    creation myth 6
    dynasties *12–13*
    emperors *11*, *12–13*
    gods and goddesses 10, 18, *19*, *22–23*, 24
    imperial palace *13*
    religions *8–9*
    rivers 8, 13, 18, *19*, *20–21*
    ships and seafaring *22–23*, *24–25*
    terra-cotta soldiers *12*
Ch'in dynasty 12, *13*
compasses, magnetic 25
Confucianism *8*, 33
Confucius *4*, *8*

daimyo 40
Di Jun 14

Ebisu 27
emperors
    Chinese *11*, *12–13*
    Japanese 29
Empress of Heaven
    (T'ien Hou) *22–23*

farming
    in China *16–17*
    in Japan *36–37*
floods
    in China *21*
    Chinese myth about *18–19*
Fuji, Mount *28*

Gemmyo, Empress 33
gods and goddesses
    Chinese 10, 18, *19*, *22–23*, 24
    Japanese *26–27*, 30–31, *34–35*, 36, *38–39*, *42–43*
    Japanese emperors as gods 45
Gonggong 18
Grand Canal *20–21*
Great Wall of China 12, *13*
Gun 18

Han dynasty 13, *17*
Han people 8
Hirohito, Emperor 45
Hiruko *26–27*
Hokkaido 28, 29
Honshu 28, 29
Huang Ho *see* Yellow River
humans, creation 6

Ise, shrine at *36*
Izanagi *26–27*, 30–31
Izanami *26–27*, 30

Jade Emperor 5, *10–11*, 12
Japan
    emperors 29, *44–45*
    farming in *36–37*
    flag 45
    gods and goddesses *26–27*, 30–31, *34–35*, 36, *38–39*, *42–43*
    islands *26–27*, *28–29*
    merchants 37
    religions 5, 29, *32–33*
    sources of myths 33
Jomon culture *29*, 32
junks, Chinese *24–25*

Kagutsuchi 30
kami 5, *32*
karma 9
katana 40
Kojiki (book) 33
Kuan Yin *9*
K'uei Hsing 10

K'ung Fu-tzu *see* Confucius
Kusa-nada-Hime 38
Kusanagi 38, *39*, 42–43
Kyushu 28

Lao-tzu 10
leech child *26–27*

Meiji, Emperor 45
merchants, Japanese 37
Minamoto clan 45
Minamoto Yoritomo *45*
Ming dynasty 13
Mongol dynasty 13

Naruhito *44*
Nihon Shoki (book) 33
Ninigi *42–43*, 44–5
Nu Wa 6

Okuninushi 42, *43*
Onogoro 26, 28

Pan Ku 6, 7
Polo, Marco *25*

Qi 18
Qing dynasty 13
Queen Mother of the West 10, 14

reincarnation 9
rice *17*, *36–37*

sampans 24
samurai 33, *40–41*
    swords *40–41*
sea, Chinese goddess of the *22–23*, 24
seppuku 40
Shang dynasty 12
Shih Huang-ti *see* Cheng, Emperor
Shikoku 28
Shinto 5, 29, *32–33*, 36
shoguns *45*
Song dynasty 13
spirits, Japanese *see kami*
Sui dynasty 13, 20

sun(s)
    Chinese myth about 14, *15*
    Japanese myth about 34, *35*
Susano-wo 31, 32, 34, *35*, 42, 45
    and the dragon's sword *38–39*
Suseri-Hime 38, 42

Takamagahara 26, 34
Tang dynasty 13
Taoism 9
terra-cotta soldiers *12*
Three Gorges dam *21*
Tiandi 18
T'ien Hou 22, *23*, 24
torii 32, *33*
Tsuki-yomi 31, 32, 35

Ukemochi *34–35*, 36

Wu Di, Emperor 16

Xi He 14
Xi Wangmu 10, 14

Yamata-no-Orochi 38, *39*
Yamato clan 43, *44–45*
Yangtze River (Cheng) 8, *19*, 20, *21*
Yao, Emperor 14
Yayoi culture 29
Yellow River (Huang Ho) 8, 20, 21
Yi 14, *15*
yin and yang 6, 7, *9*
Yomi (underworld) 30, *31*
    hags of 30
Yong Le, Emperor 25
Yu 18, *19*
Yuan dynasty 13
Yu Huang Shang-di *see* Jade Emperor

Zen Buddhism 33
Zhang E 14
Zheng He 25
Zhong-guo 8
Zhou dynasty 12